KITOTAM

Editors: Erica Violet Lee
Lynda Monahan
Cover art: John McDonald
Book and cover design: Tania Wolk, Third Wolf Studio
Printed and bound in Canada at Friesens, Altona, MB

The publisher gratefully acknowledges the support of Creative Saskatchewan,
the Canada Council for the Arts and SK Arts.

Library and Archives Canada Cataloguing in Publication

Title: Kitotam = (he speaks to it) / John McDonald.
Other titles: He speaks to it
Names: McDonald, John, 1981- author.
Description: Poems.
Identifiers: Canadiana 20210147261 | ISBN 9781989274507 (softcover)
Classification: LCC PS8625.D646 K58 2021 | DDC C811/.6—dc23

radiant press

Box 33128 Cathedral PO
Regina, SK S4T 7X2
info@radiantpress.ca
www.radiantpress.ca

(HE SPEAKS TO IT)

KITOTAM

JOHN M^cDONALD

The poems in this collection were created across the traditional ancestral homelands of countless Indigenous peoples over many years. The author wishes to thank and honour these nations and communities for sharing their ancestral spaces with him, even if but for a moment.

CONTENTS

PART ONE
KISTAPINANIHK
(THE WINTERING PLACE)

PART 2
MASINAHIKATEW
(HE WRITES IT ALL DOWN)

This book is dedicated to Rosanna Deerchild,
For giving a moment's encouragement,
At a time when it was needed the most.

Kininaskohmitin

*"I just finished my performance, and, as I walked
off the stage, this guy came up to me and said that he was
from Melfort, which is about an hour or so west of
Prince Albert. He told me that that he'd enjoyed
my performance, but then he asked me,
'Christ, don't you have any good memories of PA?'"*

-John McDonald,
recounting his performance
at the 2006 Eden Mills Writers Festival

PART ONE
KISTAPINANIHK
(THE WINTERING PLACE)

SASKATCHEWAN RIVER BLUES

Rolling water
Cold water
Dirty water
Old water
Drinking water
Poisoned water
Your water
Water in the night
Water under ice
Water 'neath the broken bridge
Water under sky
Water where the rivers meet
Water where the Marquis died
Water where the trappers camped
Water where the preachers lied
Sandbars in the water
Sturgeon in the water
Pulp Mill dump in the water
Beaver in the water
Unfinished dam in the water
Edmonton's water
Battleford's water
History's water

Swiftly flowing water

THE DRIVE

Warm winds blow across the road
The ghosts of winter dance
Across the yellow line

I'm the only one on this road tonight
It is my kingdom
My power and my glory

This road has no curves or bends
A Saskatchewan road if ever there was one
A straight line through
The Breadbasket of the World

My car is an old one
From a simpler time when
Windows opened with a turn
And ashtrays held dirty loose change
And that radio...
Amplitude Modulation Between 2 chrome dials

Turn that knob and who knows what you will find
Out-of-town scores and golden oldies
Evangelical Jesus freaks with their
Alabama accents proclaiming
Testifying
But mostly,
It's the sweet hiss between stations
White noise in the middle of the night

BOREALIS

I remember as a kid
Hearing a story
Of a man
Who whistled at the Northern Lights

They said he was struck by lightning
As punishment

These are the Dancing Dead
And you're not supposed to whistle at them

It's been a long time
Since I heard that story

I know it's silly
But I still won't whistle
At those lights

THE FARMHOUSE

I know of an old house
Down at the end of a gravel road
The grass around it has been growing
Uncut since Diefenbaker died

Any windows it had were broken long ago
The grey boards brittle beneath
Summer suns and winter winds
Of fifty years
When December comes,
the floor piles high with the snow no one comes to clear away

Swaybacked as an old mare
Tar paper peeks out through
Missing shingles on its bent roof
Doors and walls, once square and true,
Will never go back that way

It's less work to let it stand there
Than to bring it down or burn it
slowly returning to the earth
A Stonehenge for the future

It's not alone as one might think
This old house crumbling to death
The ghosts of the land still walk its halls
And sleep on those cast-iron bed frames
sit at those warped and broken tables
In a kitchen long devoid of the smell of baked bread
Alive in the silence
Warm in the quiet
No Trespassing
Do Not Disturb

DURING THE HURTING TIMES

I miss the ritual of it all
The spark of light in the dark
The flick, the click
That first sucking breath
And how that first drag smells
A little different than the next

Outside the lobby doors
Of Hotels and No-tells
Down the steps of stage doors
And out in the parking lot
Where the school buses were
We smoked

Unspoken brotherhood of addicted lungs
Huddled like bees, fighting to breathe
That eternal search
Like miners trapped underground
Looking for a light

Sent with a note to the store as a kid
Back in the old days
Picking butts and rolling your own
A full pack and
Everyone's your best friend
During the hurting times

FIRE

Wood crackles in the flames
Smoke curling into the sky,
Makes your eyes hurt
Makes you smell like you're a brand-new pair of moccasins
Warms you, but it burns you, too
Alive, it is born, it breathes,
It needs to burn,
It feeds, breeds, needs to spread, because if it cannot,
then it will die, and
When I die,
They will feed me to it,
and I
Will crackle in the flames
And my smoke will curl into the sky
And make your eyes hurt

GROWING UP IN PA

Pale bleak sky o'er the City of Jails
Chimneys spew columns of smoke into the air
Too Goddamn cold to be outside for long
These frozen days that never seem to end

Time and again, I ask myself
Why the hell do I still live here?
The place has no future
And the past is just that

Golden memories of childhood tainted
By the knowledge of what really happened

Those days of being broke
going hungry
pulp mill smells in the air
Those days they oiled the gravel roads in town
Those days of my youth

Those good times, few though they were
Young hellions run amok in the city
Raiding crabapple trees and chokecherry bushes
Riding stolen bikes down the sidewalks
Finding treasures in garbage cans and dragging them back home

Scrounged change buying Slushes and fed into arcade games
Bottles picked for deposit returns
Punches thrown in petty scuffles
Mountain ash berries and dog shit squished into the soles of our shoes
Those days in Prince Albert

THE GARBAGE PIT

Behind my grandfather's house on the reserve
Was a pit
Dug deep into the earth
Inside a stand of poplar trees

That's where the garbage went each day
The garbage pit
Where kitchen scraps mingled with
Cardboard boxes and broken glass
The place where refuse went to die

How many times were we told not to play near it, my cousins and I?
The threat of a strap across our ass
The deterrent

But not much of one

Hard to resist it, because,
That's where the sweetest Saskatoon berries grew

I fell in once
And landed in a pile of potato peelings
The fear of the strap overtaken
By the scramble to get out
And get those damn slimy things off of me

There were only five houses
On that side of the river back then
Twenty five years have come and gone
And my grandparents both lie buried
On the other side of the river
I wonder if the Saskatoon berries grow there still

MY DEAD FRIENDS

I pass them twice a day
Three white crosses in the ditch
I nod my head each time

They are dead
Killed in a car wreck on a clear July afternoon
And I am alive
That little voice inside my head
That told me not to get into that car
I listened to it, and I breathe
No white cross in the ditch for me
I live
But I live to tell
The tale
I live
To remember

MY GRANDFATHER'S HANDS

My grandfather was a man
With giant hands
that broke the land he farmed
Hands that built his house alone
built bridges and dug ditches and trenches in Europe
His hands killed Nazi soldiers
buried those that
The Nazi soldiers killed

His hands never failed him
Not once, in 90 years

It was his mind that failed him
It was his mind that would take him
Back to the battlefields of the Second World War
Again and again

It was his mind that would make him call
His daughter by his dead wife's name
Again and again

It was his mind that made him call for my grandmother before he died

His hands never failed him
Not once

THE GUITAR

A battle-scarred case sitting
Propped up in the corner, holds an
Old traveling companion
A decorated veteran
Of a hundred one-night stands

Every nick and scratch and dent tell
A long and winding tale
Of darkened rooms and street corner concerts
bush parties and times of practice
And quiet contemplation

They tell of the hurting times, when it had
To sit, silent, in the backroom of a pawnshop

Sticky drops of beer still there from the time
That drunk threw a bottle and it broke against the wall
That night in Medicine Hat
Should have been cleaned off
But it never was

This guitar has its stories
It sings without ever striking a chord

THE PLYMOUTH

How long has it sat there?
How long
Since that engine last felt
Internal Combustion

How long has it been since someone sat behind the wheel?
since
Someone dropped it into gear?

How long has it been since that gas gauge last read "full"?
since
Someone rolled down the windows?
Since
a hand out the window surfed the wind whipping past?

How long has it been since that speedometer hit 55?
since
It hit 200 thousand miles?
Since
The windshield was cleaned and the oil checked?

How long has it been since someone turned on that radio?
since
Someone made love in the back seat?

How long has it been since life passed it by?
How long has it been since someone parked it in the bush to die?

GRAVEYARDS

There's an abandoned cemetery in the town where I grew up
It's tucked into the bushes behind the Canadian Tire

They are French Catholic graves for French Catholic dead
Very few visit, but someone mows the grass

The newest grave is dated 1956
A stillborn child
Notre ange precieux

I could show you where the bodies
Of those killed by Louis Riel are buried
They have red granite obelisks for markers,
"Killed in Action at the battle of Duck Lake"

My brother is buried there, too
Between my brother's grave and the Duck Lake dead
Are the graves of nuns and soldiers
The graves of Ukrainians and Chinese
And at least 2 millionaires
In the corner, fenced off from the rest, lie the graves of the Jewish dead
of my hometown,
Their markers covered in pebbles and rocks, in the old Jewish custom
Though very few pay their respects, anymore

Tombstones enthrall me
I find them beautiful
I always have
Although I'd never have one of my own

I make it a point to visit graveyards
When I can

One day I will
make charcoal rubbings

On acid free paper
And frame them as
Works of art
Memento mori

EIGHTS AND ACES

I have this memory of a warm summer afternoon
The day growing long,5:30 or 6:00
But the sun was still up and shining

I was sitting on a picnic table, out at Little Red River Park
Sitting there with this girl
Bob Seger was blaring out of the
Rolled down windows of her dark blue Ford
The song was a slow one, *Fire Lake*

She and I had gone to elementary school together
Grade 5 or 6, I'm not sure which
What we were smoking that afternoon has helped to blur my memory
She was sitting there, her brown hair pulled back
She was wearing those green University of Saskatchewan Huskies
sweatpants
and a Marilyn Manson hoodie
The standard uniform for girls in 1997

To our peers back then,
At least a few of them
Having sex meant you were "going out"
So I guess we were "going out"
I haven't seen that girl in 16 years, but whenever I hear *Fire Lake* now
I feel warm and high

THE VIEW

Look across the water
Look across the landscape
Look across the highway
Look across the table
Look across the football field
Look across the valley
Look across the neighbor's fence
Look across the player's bench
Look across the prison yard
Look across the river bank
Look across the parking lot
look across the pasture
look across the playground
look across the bingo hall
look across the cemetery
look across the hospital bed
look across the maternity ward
look across the crime scene tape
look across the lighted stage
look across the grandstand
look across the teacher's desk
look across a lover's breast
look across the gathered crowd
look across the sidewalk
look across the doctor's face
look across the darkened gym
look across the steering wheel

look across
how do you feel?

THE CROSS OUT FRONT

I live in a town
Where the Catholic Church burned down
Many years ago

They built a new church
Very modern for the time
But since the congregation was
Slightly older than most, and
They wished to keep a piece of the old
For the new

They took two timbers
Blackened and burned from the fire, and
In front of their new church
They erected a cross
With the burned wood

Perhaps they have never known
The connotations
A burnt cross carries
I doubt they did
But still, it remains
A burnt cross
On the front lawn of a Roman Catholic Church

They decorate it with Christmas lights each year

BAD KID

Look into eyes that
Should be innocent

they are eyes that have seen way too much
Old before their time
This young boy hardened
By a life he never asked to live

They give him hell for misbehaving
They give him hell for not sitting still
They punish the symptom
Instead of treating the reason
It hardens his heart a little more each day

They are doing the best with what they're given
But he's only one child among them all
They're there to teach
Not to parent
A role forced on them more and more each day

This boy, this child, this bad kid
I ask you-did he fall through the cracks
Or was he pushed?

WHILE THEY WERE IN KANDAHAR

Lowered flags and news reports
a mention here and there online
13 years have come and gone
since they went
"over there"

newborn babies from way back then
now sit in grade 8 classrooms
baby boomers are dying off
but back then
they were middle aged

it doesn't't seem so long ago
but they fought the Taliban
Longer than your grandfather fought the Germans

Before Facebook
Before Smartphones
Before the death of the CD and the Printed Word
Three Prime Ministers
Three Popes
And four Winter Olympics have passed
Since they went "Over There"

THE ARCADES

There was a few of them scattered
Across our town
Those magnets of childhood
With their flashing lights and cacophony of billiard balls

I knew them all, or most of them
How many tens and hundreds of dollars did I alone feed into those
machines, one quarter at a time?

There was Guys and Gals downtown
And Star Billiards on Central Avenue
Dark places, heavy with smoke and noise

And the little arcade across the street
from where the SAAN store burned down

Westside Coin Laundry
Where the smell of clean clothes was forever in the air
Its arcade was always open, but almost always empty

There were a few games in the roller rink
And there was the hole-in-the-wall arcade
Beside the movie theatre
Where we hung out before the show

There was the Wizard's Palace in the mall
But the one that I miss most of all
Across the street from my high school
We'd get high out back
And hold court within

They are all gone now
Kids don't go to arcades anymore

A CUP OF TEA

I once had a cup of tea
In the kitchen of an old log cabin
Of a woman of advanced years

She was a miserable person
in the costume of a hippie
Her rustic log cabin was honestly and truly the nicest thing about her

Sitting on the mantle of the stone fireplace
Sitting on a little easel
Was a small ceramic tile
Four inches square
It was white and blue
And it was a portrait of
Karl Marx
I wanted it, and
I considered stealing it, but didn't.
I drank my tea from a chipped china cup
And stared at the tile
And thought of the ways I could steal it
Without repercussions

Why was I drinking tea with a miserable woman?

She offered.
And I was thirsty.

ADRIAN

I have always hated my middle name
The weak and
Uninspired name that it is
A millstone, one of many
Worn 'round my neck

Too many times I have heard
Those insipid impersonations
Of Sylvester Stallone
As assholes bellow out my middle name
Yeah, as if I haven't heard THAT one before
My, are YOU a clever little fuck

For some reason
My family has always called me by my middle name
Many relatives have lived and died
Knowing me only by Adrian

It's a religious name
A Christian name,
And I am neither

A popular name among
Italian and Romanian soccer players
And I am neither

I offer it to expectant mothers
As gifts to their swollen bellies
In the hopes that they will take the name from me

MIX TAPE 1993

We are teenage basement dwellers, sitting in damp and cramped and dark downstairs places, amid bare beams and floor jacks, furnace ducts and piles of dirty laundry, boxes of Christmas decorations and kids' toys lying scattered and broken on cold cement floors and drains smelling of waste water.

Against the wall or tucked into a corner or perhaps in some small room of thin walled wood paneling would sit a bed, or just a mattress, old and stained, and next to it, a dresser, scratched and dented and covered in stickers and cigarette burns, littered with empty plastic pop bottles.

On top of the dresser stands a black ghetto blaster with a stack of cassette tapes, in and out of cases, with little pieces of paper stuffed into the notches so that they could be recorded over, as you sat by the radio, waiting for the DJ to play "Those Songs", the ones you want to play in your car or in your Walkman.

You are hoping, praying that the voice on the radio will just shut up and play the song, and not talk over the first few seconds of the song, all the while hoping you have timed it just right, that there is enough tape to record the whole song, and that the click of the tape deck stopping, like a gunshot in a quiet room, will not leave the song cut in half, creating a teasing, unfulfilling mind fuck.

In the meantime, and in between time, between commercials and bad music, you listen back to what you've just recorded, making sure that it made it to tape. Then you wait for the next song, unsure of what it will be, but you'll know you'll want it on this tape.

Waiting and waiting, you become a third-party producer, a pirate, stealing the songs from the air

PROMISES

The little hippie girl with promise in her eyes
She used to weave coloured string in the sun

Then the clouds rolled in, powdered white
The pull of that storm just too strong
To keep the promise alive
Like candles on a cake
Blow makes it all go away

And she wears it on her face
In the circles 'neath her eyes
And the scratches on her arms
And the tangles in her hair
And the silence that she keeps
Where once there was peace
Now she must watch what she says
So that he can keep his cloudy ways

In the barroom, the musicians take the stage
And the people start to sway
The pull of the music just too strong
To keep her standing still
She twirls her pale thin arms
And she closes her eyes
And she smiles a little
And for a few chords
The clock turns back a moment
The colours return and cut through the powder, white.

FOR BERNICE

We were street kids,
Disposable urchins not worth the time
Immature hooligan bastards with no respect
Except to her

We were vagrants,
homeless leeches not worth the effort
Drains on society who should go get a job
Except to her

We were Indians
Decimated and ignorant races not worth the welfare cheques
Drunken stereotypes who should go back to the Rez
Except to her

We were abused women
Terrible mothers who should have known better
Or should have been better wives and they wouldn't have been hit
Except to her

We were hungry
Lazy bums who can't afford to put food on the table
Always looking for a handout
Except to her

We were inmates
Criminal monsters who should be locked up forever
And kept away from the "decent" and "good" people
Except to her.

We were the addicted
Diseased junkies who deserve what they get
Drug pushing monsters who make the streets unsafe
Except to her

We were prostitutes
Whores and loose women who are filthy and slutty
Who sell their bodies to whomever comes along,
Except to her

The fragile ones in Prince Albert's shadows
The dirty little secrets
The sordid characters of this
Gateway to the North

To us, she was Mama Bear
Our voice
Our defender
Our war chief
Sometimes our last link
To whatever makes us human beings
Sometimes our last link
To life itself

We are the chorus
The multitudes of street people and brown people and beaten people
Of young people and poor people and hungry people
Of people behind bars and people hiding behind bedroom doors
And people trading this for that
But we are people
And she knew that
And she never let us forget that
Because she never forgot

She gave life to Shauna, Mike and James
But she saved so many more.
She sacrificed herself
Worked her body and spirit to the end
For us
Not because she had to
But because others wouldn't

There are those among us
Who should not be here
Not with the cards life dealt to them
But they are here because she didn't fold
But went all in for them

I should know,
I'm one of them

THE DANCE

I watched you pierce your flesh
I watched you draw your blood
Upon the altar, dark
The priestess made her mark

Inside the minds of fools
One never knows the way
You step on broken glass
Those prayers you never say

Verses read at night
Before you go to sleep
Will not create those dreams
Secrets that they will not keep

The snow begins to drift
Those virgin piles of white
Scatter upon them dirt
But do it out of spite

Dancing the Medicine Dance
Twirling in the wind
You don't know when to stop
I'm not sure where to begin

THE SCREAM

My tires locked up
As I slammed on the brakes
The car began a sickening drift
As I tried to stop
On that gravel road
Out in the middle of nowhere

When the world finally came to a stop
Car straddling the road
Bumper deep in the tall grass in the ditch
I could hear a bellowing scream

It filled the car
And it was a few moments before
I realized
That the screaming was coming
From me

IMMATURE

These walls close in
Around my dreams again
Spin me around
Where it lands is where the truth spills out

I was young and dumb
Never thinking before speaking
Going out of my way to disturb
Hoping that you'd get the joke

I'm not the one who needs to grow up
I'm old before my time

SMOKE

There is smoke in the air again
Faint, just on the edge
The smell of burning trees

A world on fire
Stampeded by
Too much fuel
Too much heat
Too much wind
Too little rain

Smokey the Bear,
His arm upraised,
Shows us the risk

Smoke has become the smell of summer
Connected in my memory
Erasing sweet scents of
Lilacs and poplar trees
Ozone rain on wet hot pavement
Bug spray and sunscreen
Canola ripening in the fields

Those smells must be gone
Because all I seem to smell
Is smoke

LIGHTSKINNED

There are times when ours is the hardest road to walk
We will always be
The Outsiders
The reminders of colonization
The living proof that
Someone in our family
Dared a moment of passion
With a white person
Or had it forced upon them

It's what makes us
The fiercest of warriors

We are not fighting for them

We are fighting
For ourselves

OBSERVATIONS OF AN EMPTY SCHOOL

Ticking clocks
Hour hand
Minute hand
Racing each other 'round the face
Day after day
Until the battery dies

Doors rattle
Whenever the furnace kicks in
Filtered forced air
Pushed through dirty vents

Fluorescent light bulbs
Light up with a clunk
After they flicker and click
Only to buzz
Like a swarm of houseflies
Headache inducing
Nauseating
Painting the skin four different shades of pale

The distant hiss of urinals flushing
Of bells ringing
Marking recesses and lunch hours
empty classrooms
Empty playgrounds
And neighbouring houses

This building is empty
This building is filled

NORTHERN PEOPLE
(Northern Saskatchewan Fires 2015)

We're Northern people
Shaped in
Mother Nature's own forge

We're Northern people
We watch the land vanish around us
For months at a time
Under mountains of snow
While cowardly birds
Flee for southern safety

We're Northern people
By choice or tradition
We dwell within a furnace
Lit by the gods at their whim

We're Northern people
Resilient and stubborn
Soot-stained and frozen
Bug-bitten and sunburned
Surviving in your summer playground
Stewards of a land most ancient
Tough as the granite shield
Beneath our feet

It'll take more than the elements
To break us

ODE TO THOSE KILLED FEBRUARY 11, 2015
(for Michael Green, Michele Sereda,
Lacy Morin-Desjarlais and Narcisse Blood)

Bad news travels fast, old friends
Dear friends
Two thousand pounds of emotions
Like the crash that took you from us

Old friends, dear friends
Those voices, your voices
Silenced in a moment's chaos
All you have seen
Vanished in an instant
Sights stolen, experiences stolen
Every sunrise and sunset seen by your eyes
Every birdsong and drumbeat heard by your ears
Evaporated like breath
In cold winter air
With the empty hope that
It happened quickly

What foul, primal black sentiment!
To hope that a friend's death was quick?
The hope that they felt no pain?
Such pragmatic thoughts gall me
To wish a swift death!

Christ almighty, we want them to live!
To walk through that door and to say
"Sorry we're late, the roads were bad"

Old friends, dear friends
Those of us left behind
Selfish as we are
Not merely satisfied with the work you left behind
We want more
We are wanting
Wanting your bodies to come alive again

Wanting you here with us
Not in spirit
Alive
Living flesh and blood
Beating heart
Breathing lungs
Intact, whole
Alive

Old friends, dear friends
I cannot wish you rest
Because I don't believe in wishes
Any more than I believe in resurrection or in god
I can only lament your death like
A lone highland bagpiper
In pain
In loss
In grief

WHY I DO WHAT I DO

We need
to keep holding up that mirror
to those people
who are willing
to further themselves
at the expense of others

If they break the mirror,
they've done nothing
but take one mirror
and turn it into
thousands of
little mirrors

Either they change
or they prove themselves liars
for denying
what is reflected

This is the medicine of the looking glass.

SO SICK OF BEADS

When people hear the words
"Native American Art,"
a flood of images
often fills the mind

paintings of
eagle feathers
buffalo skulls
 Haida masks
 Kokopelli
moccasins
powwow regalia
dreamcatchers
The End of the Trail

 Sounds of
wooden flutes or
 DUM DUM dum dum
 DUM DUM dum dum

Bastardized souvenirs
Beaded cigarette lighter cases
Beaded Nike symbol chokers
Beaded lanyards
All these beads
Everywhere
beads beads beads

In the 70's
Beaded headbands
The sacred symbol
Of that venerated tribe
The Hollywood Indian
Created to keep braided wigs
On the heads of extras and stuntmen
As they rode across Utah and Arizona
Geronimo's land

While dressed like Sitting Bull

Goddamn colonial trinkets
Reminders of poor real estate deals
On Manhattan Island
The Death of the Red Man's way of life
Brought about by beads
This was one trinket
I had thought
Whose time had passed
since they started hiring
Real Indians
for movies
but no...
been shopping for a
Halloween costume lately?

WHY ARE WE UPSET?

We are fractured people
learning a fractured culture second-hand
put together with
bits and pieces of
what colonization
missed with the dustpan
and taught to us by
equally fractured teachers
who have to do the best they can
with what they have
and patch the holes
with plastic pony beads
from Wal-Mart
while being led by power-hungry Chiefs and Councils
with dollar signs in their eyes
and big new shiny Ford Trucks

like tourists
we learn the teachings of the Red Road
through trinkets and
Pendleton blankets
trying to become
The stoic, bucolic
Red Indians
Of the movies

Wouldn't you be mad?

RECORD STORE DAY

20+ years
buying case lots of LPs
at auctions and garage sales and thrift stores

rifling through piles of
musty, dog-eared albums
seeing more copies
of "Sunshine and Roses" by Nana Mouskouri
and those Goddamn
Funk and Wagnalls "Family Library of Great Music" classical albums
than any human should have to

all to build up
a solid enough album collection

Carting around
45 lb boxes
Of 33 rpm albums
Whenever moving house
Holding on to records
Kept for only one song
Never even listening
To the rest of the album
Dragging home filthy cabinet record players
With faux wood panelling
And burlap mesh over the tinny speakers
Much easier than
Finding replacement needles

All just to hear it on vinyl

ON THE DEATH OF JACK CENNON, JANUARY 29, 2016

I was eight years old
It was Grade Two
Princess Margaret School
Mrs. Dueck's class.

I had written a poem
for Remembrance Day

Someone sent it in
to CKBI Radio.
Next morning
I'm in the Orpheum Building
above a place that was known
as Tu-Bac-O Square

I'm ushered into a control room
and introduced to
this big eared old man
whom I vaguely recognized
from a TV commercial
for a pharmacy
where he played
both a baby
and an old man in a bathrobe who gets a face full of baby powder

He introduces me
I read my poem on the air
"The Wake-up, Shake-up Show"
my first media spot
my first performance.

So long, Jack.

MEDITATION ON THE REZ

The Rez is Open Custody
Masquerading and passed off as "our land"

There is a perimeter fence surrounding it
Razor wire and stone
It is not sunk into the earth
It is within the mind
Set stone by stone
Link by link
Generation after generation
Reinforced little by little every day
The belief that
This is all there is to the world

PART 2
MASINAHIKATEW
(HE WRITES IT ALL DOWN)

THE BUSKER

19 years old
But I had been around
My world so much bigger
Than this little hometown

With a twenty-dollar bus ticket
That could take me anywhere
In a black leather jacket
I could make my way out there

Bright Lights Big City
On the other side of night
See the skyline looming
In the dawn's early light
Greyhound station 7:30
In the AM
I light a cigarette as I step outside
Big sky open wide

Now I'm standing on a corner
Singing songs to earn your change
It's a step up from begging, but
 In your eyes
It's all one and the same

Dreaming those big dreams
In the Valley of the Kings

THE CALL

The phone woke me from a sleep
A dream of innocence so deep
That even angels stopped to weep
And you said to me

You're back in town, you just rolled in
Its half past four, "Can you come and get me?"
You're standing by the liquor store
The creeps are out, and they're looking.
You want my rescue

As if I had forgotten
Why you left in the first place
I stop you as you start to beg

You're asking way too much of me
A secret that I just can't keep
How dare you lay this at my feet
Like I can change things as I please?

What makes you think I know the way?
Or know exactly what I should say?
My good advice you threw away
I learned my lesson the hard way

The phone call woke her up as well
She's worried, as far as I could tell
She asked me who was on the phone
I tell her "Someone all alone," and I meant it.

THE INSPIRATION

It's the middle of the night
And I become inspired

Shall I pick up my paintbrush or
pick up my guitar
Shall I go for pen and paper
reach for needle and thread
Grab mallet and chisel or
Shall I wake my sleeping lover or
Shall I just roll over and
Try to fall back asleep and
Let the inspiration flow back into the
Ether, unspent and wasted?

I make a deal with myself
As my eyelids begin to close,
That if I remember it by morning
I will put it down
Somehow

BYTOWN

I was there in the spring
The snow was gone, but the
Death that winter brings left the trees bare, the grass brown and the
people bundled
the streets dusted in gravel thrown on them
When they were icy sheets

I strolled down Wellington Street,
Past the limestone facades of Gothic Revival

It was my first visit to a place
I only knew of from the news and social studies class
And as the place that made the Hinterland Who's Who commercials
It was Old Canada to me

The Carillon echoed down the city canyons
Up in some belfry on Parliament Hill
I could picture someone Like Quasimodo
Hammering away at wooden handles with their bare hands

This city
This Victorian Gentleman's Club of buildings
This memorial to the honoured dead of war
To the Empire, the British Empire
Upon which the sun never set

To think that this was once a logging town
A barbaric backwoods hovel
Where loggers and gamblers and whores lived, fought, fucked and died

The tattoo on my arm has faded slightly
I got it there
In a shop on Rideau Street
My souvenir, to the grave
Of my trip to the capital

THE HUNT FOR PHILO VANCE

12 years
Spent looking, searching for a copy
Rifling through
Moldy smelling boxes of paperbacks in basements and garages
scouring the shelves of dusty used bookstores and antique stores and
little small-town libraries and little small-town grandmothers
Yard sales and book drives, eyes always open for a copy of that book

Finding someone who had even heard of it was as challenging as finding
the damn thing itself
This unknown author of the Jazz Age pretender to the Crown of Sherlock
Holmes

12 years of business cards left with slightly overweight middle aged men
with salt and pepper hair and cardigan sweaters and bifocal glasses
"If a copy ever comes in, please call..."

In some tiny library in Southern Saskatchewan
It was there,
In 1920's splendor
This dated and politically incorrect tome
Full of racist words that make me cringe
Needing to reconcile that it was part of the story,
And acknowledging the pain of it

Although I knew the story, learned from William Powell and Mary Astor
in black and White
I read it, savored it as if it was the first time I had heard the tale
And at half past three in the morning, as I read those last few words and
closed the book I lay there, spent and sated, like I had just made love
It has been too long since a book has done that to me.

THE CANVAS

It stares at me
This barren, godforsaken landscape
Mocking me, goading me
"c'mon," it seems to say,
"Mark me"

I draw my knife into the mess of paint
I take a deep breath
It's like this each and every time
It stares at me
Pure, innocent, virginal
And I am about to deflower it
Will it be desecration
Or rapture?

The first marks are nervous stuttering lines
Hesitation marks
But the mark is made
No going back, now

The tempo builds
Rhythmic slashes and drags and draws
As I scrape the mess across its textured skin
Over and over
The fantasy taking shape with each
Thrust and parry
As I fence with emptiness
The building excitement
Rising to a climax

The knife drops from my trembling hands
And clatters to the floor
Splattering the mess in all directions

ON THE DEATH OF MAYA ANGELOU, MAY 24, 2014

On the morning they said you died
I read one of your poems to
A group of Grade Three students

I asked them what a poet was
"a poet is someone who writes poems"
One said

I smiled and asked,
"what is a poem?"

"those are what poets write,"
Came the reply

Innocent, ignorant minds
Growing up in a world where
Reading is a chore
Not a joyful escape

On the morning they said you died
I feared the loss
Of what went with you

ON THE DEATH OF MR. DRESSUP, SEPTEMBER 2001

We were drawn to him as children
With wit and smiles and song
Cloaked in borrowed clothes and fables of old
From the Tickle Trunk
To the open souls of the young

Our lunch hour ritual
Filled with his friendly guises
He played muse to our infant minds
Spilling knowledge into our eyes

Had not the Twin Towers fallen seven days before
It would be him we would be lamenting
In a national brow of sorrow

The Tickle Trunk sits silent now
The treehouse lights are dim
Gone now is the magic
Magic ink
From a now empty well

CANADIAN SKIN

Swath yourself in ecstasy
O you of Canadian skin
Yours is an existence
Where the role is cast
In the eye of the globe

Your reputation precedes by decades
An open diary
to the countryman
of the lorry driver
Who delivered your luggage
To a village you've never been to

Born of the fetid muck of battle
And baptised in the Hollywood Hills
The truths read as scripture
Of serge and horse and Northwest Mounted
Feral domain and polar display
Kind and polite and our "ohs" like "oohs"
The bride of truth veiled in ignorance

Tread softly onward
O you of Canadian skin
The overcoat fits nicely
Worn with ease
But the warm winds of change shift
And the comforting cloak woven long before
Will be too warm,
too much to bear
O you of Canadian skin

ODE TO TOM THOMSON

The man was a painter
The man painted trees
The man was a woodsman
The man lived with trees
The man was a canoeist
The man paddled by trees
The man was found dead in Algonquin Park
The man died by trees
The man was in the water
The man drowned by trees
The man was buried in Algonquin Park
The man was buried by trees
The man became Canadian Myth
The man known for painting trees

MESSIAH

Upon my word
They walked to the edge
Upon my word
They peered over
Upon my word
The others pushed them
And for a moment
They envied the birds

In my mind's eye
The lines were perfect
In my mind's eye
The colours stood true
In my mind's eye

It took her breath away
And for a moment
I was a master

At the crescendo
They swayed in ecstasy
At the crescendo
They dipped and they twirled
At the crescendo
Their bodies melded into one
And for a moment
They became the night

As the houselights went out
The sweat rolled down
As the houselights went out
I closed my weary eyes
As the houselights went out
I vanished from the audience
And for a moment
The character is dead

UNTITLED NO. 8 OR 9

We stand in the limelight of the gods
Have we made the most of our time here?
What shall we bring to this table?
Smile, you bastards!

We are the spoils of enterprise
We are the lamentations of decay
We were all one in the purest sense
the message has been lost
and we must accept it?

Ours was a journey to join
and we as mortal men have failed
We were to come together in a massive wave,
Pure and unabashed in our minds
Our slates were to have been wiped clean
with the waters of the earth

Instead we have drowned ourselves
Divided we stood, united we fall
The pile of the many
a vast chasm of loss exists
Where a pillar of strength should have been,
Gleaming immaculate in the summer sky

The gods and dogs weep for us
Pass the torch onto the children
Perhaps they may stand where we have tumbled
May they stand not merely as a collective mass
But as the prototype of hope,
as one sentient being
truly interdependent upon its constituent parts

AT THE FEET OF THE STATUE OF ATHENA

Tell me something
Tell me anything
Don't just stand there
Staring at me silently
Speak
Say something
Anything

You know damn well
That silence annoys me
It gnaws at my soul
Peeves and perturbs me
Grates upon my nerves
Speak

It's been years
Too many years
Since I first came
To sit by your feet
And stare into your downcast eyes
Kiss the tops of your feet
And caress the edges of your cloak
Speak
Please

I have to go now
They are closing the doors
This is your last chance
To speak

TIME

Give me a second and I'll write you a thought
Give me a minute and I'll write you a verse
Give me an hour and I'll write you a poem
Give me a day, and I'll write you a novel
Give me a week and I'll write you an epic
Give me a month and I'll write you history
Give me a year and I'll write you mythology
Give me time, and I'll make magic

FOR ALLISON

I once saw you walking
In quiet contemplation
Down cobblestones once travelled
By the feet of ancient princes
And my soul cried out in rapture
For it alone had witnessed
The pull of unseen hands
That began to draw together
You and I

And though your eyes have gazed
Upon the majesty of nature
I would hope that when you join me
On this everlasting journey
You will take my hand and hold your breath
A gamble upon every step
And if we end with nothing left
May we leave with no regret
Toss the dice against the odds
We shall testify before the gods
That this day
We have become
Children in the morning light
Rub our eyes and wonder
Each rising of the sun and moon
The veil of what it truly means
To love

And as my body falls under the hand of time
Remember this, my love
Upon my soul
Written in stone
Your name, everlasting
A leap, a step
A dare

ON LANGUAGE

Words stitched together
In particular cadence
Meant to be read in
This particular way
Be it out loud
Or silently in your head

It is odd that
So much of these
Various combinations of the
Twenty six letters of
The English language
Are manipulated to
Increase emotional connectivity

And,
What of all those words
Birthed upon
Lined sheets of paper
Or pixelated computer screens
The words that do not
Meet the requirements and
Are torn from coil ring binders
Or
Select All...Delete
Eradicated from existence
Their only crime having been
Not a good enough combination
Of those twenty-six letters

Those combinations
Compiled like
A spoonful of alphabet soup
Or tiles from a scrabble board

Joined
Married
Consecrated

These straight lines
Curlicues
Whirls, swirls and dots
A ciphered code

There's more than a few of us
 first taught this code
sitting in front of television screens
as Big Bird and Grover
Bert and Ernie
Indoctrinated us into
This cult of mysteries
And taught us the incantation,
The sacred song of knowledge
abcdefghijklmnop

Those hieroglyphics
We stared at from our school desk
As they hung upon the walls
Written in chalk at the very top of
The blackboard

Letters
Vowels and consonants
The dying art of words
Being slaughtered by
Abbreviated phrases
Like Huxley's Brave New World

This Nu-Speak
With its LOLs and OMGs
And with a generation that
Cannot write in cursive
And cannot read anything handwritten

What would Big Bird say if he could see us now?

DÉJÀ VU

Blast from the past
Looking older
Somewhat rounder
Still confounding

Intertwined
With aggravation
Deep appreciation
Angry hostility
Repressed memory

The cause of
So much poetry
Sleepless nights
Unsent letters
Hang-up phone calls
Gossamer trust
Underlying lust
Naïve desire
I once built a Lodge of Glass 'round her

Poor investment of emotions
Deeper that it should have been
Should've been a winter's fling
Undeserved devotion
Blinders to the truth
Ignoring reality

The setup for cascading system failure
Burning up on re-entry
Crashing into the ocean
Flames quenched
Hot to the touch
Blistering truth lanced and drained
Itching as it heals

ODE TO ZIGGY STARDUST

She shook me awake this morning
"He's dead," she said
"Who?" said I
"The One," she replied

He was more than just one
He was many

The spangled gleaming light at the end of the tunnel
The dapper lothario
In the dark recesses of the club
The foppish, prancing switch
Which no gay-basher could slag
Personified in crimson light

For this I loved him
In my own silent way
The one who sang for me
The one who sang to me

Now I curl up in my memories
And cry myself to sleep

FIDGET

Tired eyes
Sleepy minds
Sluggish movement
Quiet words

Silent bodies
Silent halls
Soft footsteps

Apathy
Ignorance
Lackluster
No desire
Don't want to be here
Lethargy
Immaturity
Naïve immortality

Blank stares at
Blank pages
Yawning mouths
Tapping fingers
Tapping feet

Contradiction of tired bodies
Wound tighter than a rubber band....

INSOMNIA

Water ticking in the pipes
Keeping time with my pulse
Tap tap tap

Eyes staring at the peeling paint
(chained to the rules)
Fingers drumming on my chest
(like a dog to a tree)
Dry tongue trying to wet my lips
(you must write this)
Dry eyes nailed open wide
Mind racing
Wishing

The poet muzzled
The words stifled
Inspiration rampant, but
Overridden
Juxtaposition
Cool pillows turning warm
Alarm clock sitting like a waiting bomb
Always darkest before the dawn
(Insomnia)

RAGNAROK 2015
(the purging of unfinished paintings)

I burn them
For they are mine to burn

They were like dreams
Vivid while dreaming
But forgotten upon waking
Seen, then gone

I burn them
So that I may see
Paint bubbling and blistering
Like pale skin in the sun
Distorting, collapsing
Toxic chemical fumes igniting
Flashing over
The flames painting their own colours
Green and blue and yellow

I burn them at night
To make the coyotes howl around me
Disturbance of the cool darkness
Fire always disturbs the prairie

Unwanted, unfinished
Uninspired streaks of pigment
Half-hearted glimpses
Burned
Returned

WITH MIGUEL

It was around 8 or 9 as I walked down the sidewalk with Miguel

The sun was setting and the shadows were getting longer
As everything took on an orange glow

The sounds and smells coming out of the restaurants and bars along
the street were colliding with the sounds and smells of the cars
crawling east
Towards the hills and away from downtown

The places along this street were all ethnic- Cuban restaurants
Vietnamese restaurants, Soul food joints and Hole-in-the-wall spots
with signs written in colourful languages unknown to me, a Cree kid
from the middle of nowhere.

Miguel shook a few hands as we walked, his burgundy silk dress shirt
looking like copper in the setting sun, his guitar was squeezed tightly
by the neck in his left hand.
He switched it back and forth, trying to avoid smacking it against the
parking meters and lampposts.
When he switched the guitar from hand to hand, once or twice, our
fingers would meet for a moment and intertwine, the closest we came
to a public display.

We walked past the doors of what was once a clothing store, the glass
display windows long ago boarded up and painted a dark chocolate
brown, covered with staples, tape and the remnants of God knows how
many posters and flyers.

A door opened, and a little Vietnamese man stepped out, short, balding
and fifty.
He wore a white short sleeve dress shirt and wheat-coloured slacks,
dark sunglasses shielding his eyes.

He lit the cigarette dangling from his lips.

He recognised us both. "Hey," he called out, "How are you guys doing tonight?"

We smiled said we were doing fine. Miguel brushed a stray hair from his face.

Our friend's name was Tim. He was one of the Boat People, and he was proud of that.

He took a drag off his smoke. He asked what we were doing.

We told him we were wandering, maybe looking for a drink or a bite to eat, but nothing solid as of yet.

Tim smiled. He looked at Miguel, whose soft dark skin and long black hair in his purple shirt might have gotten us beaten up in the bars down by the bus station.

"You know," Tim said through a lungful of smoke, "Maria is looking to hire a player."

"What happened to what's his name?" we asked, as I watched as a little old man stepped out of the corner liquor store.

"He quit," Tim said.

Miguel asked me, "What do you think?"

Reminded of my thirst, I replied, "It's up to you."

Miguel nodded. He said we'd go talk to Maria, and we headed west, back into the setting sun.

ON THE DEATH OF LEONARD COHEN, NOVEMBER 7, 2016

last night I lay in a darkened room
listening to your voice as
it soothed me through
what is
a very dark time in my life
right now

It crossed my mind
but for a split second-
maybe I shouldn't listen to this
right now
maybe the curse of 2016
will strike again

But I did
and it has

You have gone.
Journeyed to the Tower of Song
to join the others
you sang about -
Hank Williams
Janis Joplin
Suzanne

I hope she's waiting there
with Tea and Oranges
that came all the way from China.

The pages now fall from the spine
Yellow, brittle
Like autumn leaves
To land upon
Wet sodden earth
To return to
The pulp from whence they came

Those printed words
Though still legible,
The ink begins to smear and run
Like mascara from
A woman's crying eyes

Merci beaucoup, mon ami

Thank you for
Inspiration
Contemplation
being
the Canadian poet
all Canadian poets
want to be

Au revoir and hallelujah

EASTER SUNDAY

Easter Sunday always reminds me
Of all of us who lost so much-
Our language
Our culture
Our freedom

So many
Still shackled to the faith
That wanted to kill us

I do not think of the man who died on the cross
I think about the thousands who died
Because of the Cross

IN AN OLD MOTEL

In an old motel
I sat cross-legged on the floor
With my eyes fixed on the floor
In an old motel
On the outskirts of this town

Spilled word
Half-birthed ideas
Lying dormant inside an electric memory palace
In an old motel
False memories
Imagined words
Created by me in the dead of the night
In an old motel
Wild oats sewn in vain, altruistic hope
That they might take root and grow

In an old motel
Even these messy words
Scribbled in my messy handwriting
Are written in a 20-year-old
Long-form notebook
Purchased in a small shop in England
Bought long ago
A notebook kept in the hope that
You will, one day,
"write something"

In an old motel room
I sit cross-legged on the floor
With my eyes fixed upon the door
This ancient notebook in my hand
On the outskirts of this town

UNPLUGGED

Waltz through the ashes like an Agony Aunt
To the tired refrains of your song
For you know you're the cause of this new-dying fire
I suspect that you've known all along

Barefoot guitar player
Electric axe unplugged
Rusty strings plinking out songs of lost glories
Callouses on fingertips long gone
The thin metal strings bite and draw blood
Like a first-time seamstress

You show the disdain of a much-older cat
When approached by a young interloping kitten
A warning gaze
Then look away
But still keeping watch
Out of the corner of the eye

WINTER GARBAGE FIRE

Flames burn through black plastic bag
Discarded jack of diamonds illuminated before catching fire
As the flames turn the twilight blue snow orange
Rising heatwaves lift cardboard ash into the air
And scatter it across the untouched snow like a wasp's nest
Kicked apart as the last of them die.

Sizzling melting plastic drips into melted snow

More snow is headed our way
This winter
Unending as it is
Holding back the hopes of spring
I wouldn't begrudge a mosquito's buzz right now
Any sign of life is welcome

A TOUCH OF INSPIRATION

Words come rarely these days
But when they do
By god, you must be ready to write them down
Before they run away
Make sure your net has no holes

AN ODE TO THE FIDDLER
(for Tristen Durocher)

Therein lies the fiddler,
The Northerner,
Sitting in the shade of the man-made trees near the man-made lake,
635 kilometers south
Of where the trees and waters were there first.

Therein lies the fiddler,
His tea growing cold in his ceramic mug
As the sun takes the shadow of his lodge,
The shadows of the photographs around it,
And stretches them far across the man-made lawns
So precious to the ones with the guns and badges

Therein lies the fiddler,
Smiling the tired smile of a warrior spirit
As people come for their photo ops
And clamour to be
On the "right side of all this"

Therein lies the fiddler,
Upon his heart the spirits of young ones
Upon whose caskets and urns
The notes of his fiddle fell upon too many times

Therein lies the fiddler,
Speaking for those who cannot speak for themselves,
Outside of a building full of people who will not listen,
Fighting a battle for a world where young people will
Not have to see the end of a rope as a solution,
Upon land where Riel was subjected to such a solution

Therein lies the fiddler,
Like the warriors of old
Hungry spirit, hunger strike
Upon the prairies where trees never grew

Therein lies the fiddler,
His medicine bundle overflowing,
Overflowing like the circles of photographs around his lodge

Therein lies the fiddler

TRAVELLER

Sit here by my fire
Warm yourself, and
Share your stories
You have come all this way,
So, there's no use staying silent
What do you bring to the fight?
What words of wisdom can you teach?
We need yours now, more than ever before
Rest, if you need to
Take the chill from your bones
But, in the daylight,
Be prepared to speak, for we go at dawn

WALKABOUT IN TREATY FOUR TERRITORY

I got out of the car to stretch my legs
At the place where Highway 2 ends

The Summer smell of Southern Saskatchewan is strange to me

I stop to pick buffalo sage on this bald, parched prairie
The wind takes my tobacco offering and
Blows it towards the eighteen wheelers thundering eastbound past me

I turn to face north.
The ribbon of asphalt at my feet stretches from here to La Ronge
400 kilometeres down this stretch lies
The turnoff to my house

I feel suffocated by the open land
I need trees

ROUNDS

Every cannon ball fired,
Every shell, every anti-aircraft round,
Every direct hit or shell-splash miss,
Every curtain of flak
Every round of ammunition fired
By sailing ship, pirate ship,
Dreadnought, battleship
U-boat and Corvette
Fighter plane and Kamikaze
Since the dawn of the age of armed sail,
Still lies at the bottom of the sea
The ocean floor is littered with
Billions of bullets

SASKATCHEWAN

The winter winds still blow here,
Harsh and cold against the bald prairie
Any sense of warmth is stolen
And buried beneath deep snow

It's our usual "six months of this,"
Half of year devoid of life
Devoid of green grass and leaves
And the summer's unadulterated sun.

I miss the sun,
I miss the warmth of the sun upon
My black t-shirt
And the smells of sunscreen and bug spray
The cold winter kills any love I have for this place
Although there is very little love left.

I find myself searching for other places
For a kinder, less hateful place
In the hopes that it must be out there,
Somewhere

THE DOG SOLDIERS

We are the warriors
We are the Dog Soldiers
We defend, to the bitter end,
The people.
Our words are our weapons.
We stole them from the fort.
We use these weapons
We stake ourselves to the ground with them
Otacimawak
The storytellers
We speak for our dead
We speak and we fight
For those
Awiyak eka kohpehtakosowenit
Voiceless

THE TAG

Paint can rattles in the trainyard night
Hissing metal snakes spitting venom on
Cold rounded steel
My finger drips solid black
Spattering the blood of the can in quick, measured strokes

Curled random shapes
Twenty feet long
Multicoloured chaos tied together
With ribbons of black enamel

The hairs in my nostrils stiff from the fumes
Like cold air on a winter's day
What colour will my snot be tomorrow?

Solid masses splattered
Oblong distorted lettering
Scrawled across the belly of the train car
Thrown quickly, quickly
One step ahead of the cops
Ready to drop
And leave behind
Unfinished epitaphs
That will say nothing

Need to finish
Bend my back to reach the bottom
Rattle rattle, the can
In my hand
Agitator in can, agitator on steel train car sides
Gawked at by those
Waiting at crossing signals
Watching the work
Mine, his, hers, theirs
Rolling past
Muttering that they can't read what it says

But they all say the same thing
I was here
This is my mark
I was here.

John McDonald is a Nehiyawak-Metis multidiscipinary writer and artist from Prince Albert, Saskatchewan. He is from the Muskeg Lake Cree Nation and the Mistawasis Nehiyawak. The great-great-great grandson of Chief Mistawasis of the Plains Cree, as well as the grandson of famed Metis leader Jim Brady, John's writings and artwork have been displayed in various publications, private and permanent collections, and galleries around the world. John is the author of several books, and has had his work published and presented around the globe. He studied at England's prestigious University of Cambridge, where, in July 2000 he made international headlines by symbolically 'discovering' and 'claiming' England for the First Peoples of the Americas. John is an acclaimed public speaker, who has appeared at the Anskohk Aboriginal Literature Festival, the Black Hills Seminars on Reclaiming Youth, The Appalachian Mountain Seminars, the Edmonton and Fort McMurray Literary Festivals, the Eden Mills Writers Festival and at the Ottawa International Writers Festival. John was included in the Aboriginal Artists and Performers Inventory for the 2010 Olympic Winter Games in Vancouver, BC., his artwork and writing have been nominated for several awards, and he has been awarded several grants from SK Arts. A noted polymath, John lives in Northern Saskatchewan.